USING THE INNER ART OF DOWSING
IN THE SEARCH OF MY LIFE'S PATH—SOUL MISSION

Anneliese Gabriel Hagemann

Published by 3 H Dowsing International
Printed in U.S.A., Palmer Publications, Inc., 318 North Main Street, Amherst, WI 54406

Library of Congress Catalog Card Number 99-90656
Special thanks to Gabriella Kemp who typed and edited this material.

Address: 3 H Dowsing International
3717 N Wisconsin Avenue
Florence, Arizona 85132
Tel.# 520-868-5711

Wet
Em

Email Address: ilovedowsing@hotmail.com
anneliese@3hdowsing.com
Web Site Address: www.3hdowsing.com

A loose-leaf workbook **"TO OUR HEALTH": USING THE INNER ART OF DOWSING** in the Search for HEALTH HAPPINESS HARMONY in BODY MIND SPIRIT, Written with Love, published privately by Anneliese Gabriel Hagemann and Doris Katharine Hagemann. Printed in the USA. Copyright 1996.

Revised Editions copyright 1997/1998 **"TO OUR HEALTH": USING THE INNER ART OF DOWSING** in the Search for HEALTH HAPPINESS HARMONY in BODY MIND SPIRIT. Written with Love by Anneliese Gabriel Hagemann and Doris Katharine Hagemann. Published by 3 H DOWSING INTERNATIONAL. Printed in the USA by Palmer Publications, Inc., 318 North Main Street, Amherst, WI 54406.
ISBN 0-9656653-0-5

A spiral workbook **"DOWSING / DIVINING"**:
THE GOLDEN KEY TO TAPPING ENERGIES
Written with Love by Anneliese Gabriel Hagemann, published in 1998 by 3 H DOWSING INTERNATIONAL.
ISBN 0-9656653-5-6

TO OUR HEALTH, "A QUICK GAUGE TO BODY MIND SPIRIT WELLNESS"
...IMMUNE SYSTEM BALANCER..., written with Love by Anneliese Gabriel Hagemann. Copyright 1999, published by 3 H DOWSING INTERNATIONAL. Printed in the USA by Palmer Publications, Inc., 318 North Main Street, Amherst, WI 54406.
ISBN 0-9656653-3-X

USING THE INNER ART OF DOWSING in search of
"MY LIFE'S PATH / SOUL MISSION," written with Love by Anneliese Gabriel Hagemann. Copyright 1999. Published by 3 H DOWSING INTERNATIONAL. Printed in the USA by Palmer Publications, Inc., 318 North Main Street, Amherst, WI 54406.
ISBN 0-956653-1-3

These workbooks may be purchased for educational purposes.

Cover design by Doris Katharine Hagemann.

ISBN 0-9656653-1-3

Library of Congress Number 99-90656

Table of Contents

Preface

Many, many people through workshops and private studies are using the workbook <u>To Our Health</u>, written with love by Anneliese and Doris Hagemann, published in 1996, revised in 1997/98. By clearing out obstacles from our total Being, we are now asking, **"Where do I go from here? What is my Life's Path - my Soul Mission?"** Here is the Book, <u>Using the Inner Art of Dowsing in the Search of my Life's Path - Soul Mission</u>, ready to help in the Search to fulfill our journey on this planet called Earth.

Dedication: This material is dedicated to my physical and spiritual families who are teaching me to live in God's (Universal) Truth.

Special thanks to Gabriella Kemp who spent many months going through my hand written material, typed and edited it. Without Gabriella this material would not be ready for you my family of Love and Light. Thanks again from the bottom of my heart.

Thanks to you All.
Anneliese

Who am I?

I remember who I am.
I accept that I am Whole Love - Truth
I let go of all judgment of myself and others and know that I did the best I could.
I keep my Life simple and follow my highest Path
I stay in tune with the Higher Source within me, and let it guide me.
I am gentle and kind with myself and others
I pace myself with one Step at the time
I know the perfect circumstances present themselves
for my continued growth.
I am Truth,
I am Whole Love,
I am Joy
I am Peace.

(Found on a slip of paper with no name.
Thank you to the author of this quote.)

This is the Year!

Wonderful, wonderful, fortunate you.
This is the year that your dreams come true!
This is the year that your ship comes in:
This is the year you find Love within.
This is the year you are glad to live:
This is the year you have much to give.
This is the year when you know the Truth:
This is the year when you find new youth.
This is the year that brings happiness:
This is the year you live to bless.
Wonderful, wonderful, fortunate you,
This is the year that your dreams come true!

Russell A. Kemp

Who Am I?

In my Search for my **Life's Path and Soul Mission** I need to answer this primary question,
"Who AM I?"
If I don't know Who I Am and where I am in My Life, I cannot truly begin my Journey,
my Search.

This is a time when I need to strive for honesty within my Self. I need to look at myself in all aspects - light, dark, and shadow and *respect and honor* who I am. I do not feel regrets or anger, but know that it has brought me to where I am now. The lessons I have learned along the way have been stepping stones. Even the darkest, saddest moments have held lessons for me. I realize this and accept it.

"It is not the Years that count, it is what I have done with it and learned from it." As I complete the Charts on the following pages, I answer each question as honestly as I can. I include all the various aspects of myself that come to my mind.

I am a multidimensional Being of Love and Light.
Different parts of myself come through at different moments and during different interactions with myself and/or others.
"We nee to listen to our Heart and know also that the work of Self Change is progressing in our Life."

Attitude

"The longer I live, the more I realize the impact of attitude on life. Attitude, to me, is more important than fact. It is more important than the past, than education, than money, than circumstances, than failures, than successes, than what other people think or say or do. It is more important than appearance, giftedness, or skill. It will make or break a company...a church...a home. The remarkable thing is we have a choice every day regarding the attitude we will embrace for that day. We cannot change our past...we cannot change the fact that people will act in a certain way. We cannot change the inevitable. The only thing we can do is play on the one string we have, and that is our attitude. I am convinced that life is 10% what happens to me and 90% how I react to it. And so it is with you. We are in charge of our Attitudes."

Charles Swindoll

There is a Native American saying: **If you give a person a fish, you feed that person one meal. But if you teach a person how to fish (dowse), you feed him or her for a lifetime.**

Dowsing/Divining

Dowsing is an ancient art, known of and used by humanity for thousands of years. In the past it has been used only as a tool for finding water, but in this modern time other applications for dowsing have been explored and developed or possibly merely rediscovered. There are many different methods that dowsers use - pendulums, rods, sticks, etc. - it is up to the individual to find which method is most appropriate for them. Many people have written a variety of books on applying dowsing throughout all areas of life (see reference section in appendix).

"I know very well that many scientists consider dowsing as they do astrology, as a type of ancient superstition. According to my conviction this is, however, unjustified. The dowsing rod is a simple instrument which shows the reaction of the human nervous system to certain factors which are unknown to us at this time."

Albert Einstein

When dowsing, many feel they are tuning into their subconscious mind...a type of sending-receiving station, which is a tie between the universe and one's physical, mental, psychic self, as well as the past, present, and future. The French philosopher Theodore Simon Jouffroy said, *"The subconscious mind will not take the trouble to work for those who do not believe in it."*

Of course, there are other methods to use when working with this material. Kineseology, Intuition, Fingerstick, Hands on, Gut Feelings, etc. might be alternative approaches you may feel more comfortable with. Use them!

Learning How to Dowse
Guidelines for Dowsing

Our Higher Self, God/Universe is the Diviner
We are all naked in the Real World of Energies

1. **Protection**: You may use: A Prayer, God Force
   Your First Name
   White Golden Light
   What ever you feel the most comfortable with

2. **Let go of Ego   Embrace God (Universe)   Channel the Truth**
   write it out on a piece of paper and hold it, you may need to write it more than one time.

3. **Clean/Clear your Pendulum**
   by: Blowing on it, Rubbing it, Talking to it

4. **Find your   Yes   No   Neutral**
   If the pendulum does not want to move, give it a push. Wonder what the answer is.
   Ask questions you already know, like my name is___/s my name Karl?/I live in city.

5. **Use the word "Suppress" when needed**
   "Suppress" means pulling your Energy closer to you, especially when you are in a group
   of people experiencing interference. Write "Suppress" on a piece of paper and hold it.
   You may need to write it more than one time. Hold the paper in your hand, or put it in
   your pocket.

6. **Drink Plenty of Water** (Conductor)
   When you Dowse or when you do any kind of Energy work
   Also recommended: **Fresh Air   Food   A Walk**

7. **Breathe through your mouth - don't block your natural energy flow**
   Sometimes its helpful to put your tongue on the top behind the front teeth, to stay
   grounded, to balance, to get a clearer Yes/No

8. **May I?**   Do I have permission on all levels of consciousness?
   My consciousness   Their consciousness?
   Conscious   Subconscious   Superconscious   Unconscious   DUPI
   Soul Level of Consciousness
   If you do not have permission, talk to that CONSCIOUSNESS.

9, **Can I?**   Do I have the ability to successfully dowse in this area?   Am I ready?

10. **Should I?** Is it for the highest good of all concerned?

11. **Ask one question at a time and be very specific.** You must phrase the question so it can be answered with a yes or no movement. When the pendulum moves in many directions it means strong emotion shakes the nervous system. There are other movements you may experience such as:

   I don't know   **Not at this time**   **Don't ask this question, etc.**

12. **The Key to Accuracy in getting the correct response is using the correct words.**

13. **Practice   Practice   Practice   Practice**

14. **Be Thankful - Show Your Gratitude. K.I.S. –Keep It Simple.**

Is this in the **Highest Good?**
Mine/Family/Friends/ etc. For the Good of All?
Is my doing this for the Greatest Good of my Creator?

Ask Permission:
Am I compatible with this Being (Name)
on all Levels of Consciousness, Conscious, Subconscious, Superconscious,
Unconscious, DUPI, Soul
on all Levels of my Being Body/Mind/Emotions/Spiritual Soul
On all Levels of the (his) being

My Relationship with this Being (Name is mainly functioning on the
Physical/Mental/Emotional/Spiritual - ask %)
Look also on our chart (page 35)

Is it to my greatest/highest benefit to _____ at this time.

Examples:
House
To invest - rent, lease or buy/ car, etc.

Is it for my Highest Good to go back to School
Write down all the things (areas) you are interested in pursuing.

Is it for my Highest Good to move, year, month, etc.

Is it for my Family's Highest Good, job training, temporary job opportunity

Who Am I
The Path I Have Walked So Far

(Please use the pull-out form at the back of this book. If you have more to add, use an extra sheet of paper.)

1. Name:_____

2. Birthdate:_____

3. Telephone/FAX/email:_____

4. Address(es):_____

5. Place of Birth:_____

6. Culture/Race/Ethnicity:_____

7. Parents/Grandparents/Guardians_____

   _____

8. Siblings_____

9. Marriage/Relationships/Divorce/Separation_____

   _____

10. In-laws/significant Family Members/Blood/non-blood relations_____

    _____

11. Children (natural born, adopted, step-, god-)_____

    _____

12. Grandchildren:_____

    _____

13. Death of Significant People:_____

14. Significant People Who Have Affected You (+/-)_____

    _____

15. Religious/Spiritual Belief Systems _____

16. Health/Medical/Conditions _____

_____

17. Education (all) _____

18. Work Experience/Occupation/Career _____

_____

19. Financial Situation (savings, debts, real estate, insurance, etc.) _____

_____

20. Leisure/Hobby/Sports _____

_____

21. Places of importance/significance (-/+) _____

_____

22. Features of Society that Concern You _____

_____

23. Government/Political/Social Organizations _____

_____

24. Media/Public Relations _____

25. Violence/Crime/Abuse/Neglect _____

_____

26. Special Events/Holidays _____

_____

27. Animals/Plants/Mineral Kingdom _____

28. Past Lives - also Fears/Habits/ Patterns/Cycles/[Ego: alter, material, spiritual]_____

It may be necessary to balance some of the issues which present themselves before I can move on finding my Life's Path - Soul Mission. To do this, finish my past Journey by dowsing the pages of **Who Am I? The Path I Have Walked So Far?** and the pages that follow in which Fears, Patterns, Habits, Cycles, Ego, etc. are further explained.

Follow these steps:

1. Dowse the pages **Who Am I? The Path I Have Walked So Far**
  Question - are there any issues I need to take care of/resolve before I move on to the other pages? If yes, then you use the Issue Record Sheet (in the appendix) and start recording (an example Record Sheet is on page 12).

1a. Then Dowse Patterns = What are the Core Patterns I need to let go of? (Page 15)

1b. Then Dowse Habits = What are the Habits I need to let go of? (Page 15)

1c. Then Dowse Fear issues = What are the Fears I/we need to address and let go of? (Page 16)

1d. Then Dowse Ego's = Which Ego do I/we need to let go of? (Page 17)

Steps to follow to complete the Issue Record Balance Sheet which you pull out from the back of the book.

1. Starting with identification of the Issue. (Page 8)
2. At what level of consciousness is it blocked? (Page 18)
3. Where does the issue manifest in/on/around body? (Page 19)
4. Who is involved with the issue/ is it mine or someone else's? (Page 20)
5. When did the issue arise (time)? (Page 20)
6. What negative energy am I holding? (Pages 21-25)
7. What positive energy wants to be in place? (Pages 21, 26-28)
8. Resolution - how do I need to shift the energy to balance? (Page 30)
9. Is this issue 100% balanced? (very important) (Page 31)

Example:

1. Start with Identification of Issues by dowsing the form **"Who Am I ? The Path I have Walked so Far."** Ask the question, **"Are there any issues I need to take care of/resolve before I move on to the other pages?"** If yes, wherever the pendulum stops, ask for more information. For example, if it stopped on #15 Religious/Spiritual/Belief Systems, ask "Do I have an issue with religion? With spirituality? With Belief systems? If it stopped on religion, find out what religion it is, (you can go to TO OUR HEALTH for a list). Record the response on the Issue Record Balance Sheet, column #1 under WHO AM I?

2. Then ask on **what level of Consciousness** is this issue blocked? Dowse the options listed on page 18:

  Conscious Subconscious Superconscious Unconscious

  DUPI   Soul Level of Consciousness

  If, for example, "Subconscious" came up, enter that in column 2 Level of Consciousness.

3. Then find out "**Where is this issue manifested** (page 19). If it, for example, showed up as Sensory Organs then record sensory organs (ears) in column 3

4. **Who** is involved with this issue Go to page 20.
Record this in #4 Who. For example, if it is a female find out who it is, mothcr sister ,etc.? Also ask if it is my issue? someone else's issue? our issue? and record that.

5. **When did this issue arise**? More than one year ago? If yes, then jump to more than 5 years ago. If not then go down in time frame - less than 11 months, 10 months, etc. Record the time in Column #5.

6. What **Negative Energy** am I holding on this issue. Go to page 21, 22-25. Find out the energy and record on #6A Negative Energy. In general, search for the most important energy vibration which wants to go.
What **Positive Replacement Energy** wants to be in you? Go to page 21, 26-28 and record in column #6B. Find the most important positive energy vibration.

7. **Resolution** = How does this issue want to be balanced? Go to page 29 for resolutions. Dowse out and record. It is advisable to write it out first:

This is my/their/not my/ issue. I let go of the **___negative energy)___** **which is held on my**
____(level of consciousness)__ level of my being and manifested in my _____. This
energy no longer serves me. I am now feeling ____(positive energy)_____. Bless Love,
Bless Love, Bless Love, etc.

8. **THE ENERGY HAS TO BALANCE 100%**. You ask, "Is this issue 100% balanced?" If it says no, find another negative vibration/word to let go of, or a positive vibration word to replace it with. Or you might need to write more Bless Love until it is 100% balanced. **This is the Key**. Otherwise the energy grows again.

Example
Issue Record Balance Sheet

Name: ___Anneliese Hagemann___ Birthdate ___9/11/36___ Address ___W10160 County Road C Wautoma WI___ Phone ___920-787-4747___

Follow steps 1-9 Pages 13-14	Page 18	Page 19	Page 20	Page 20	Page 21	Page 21	Page 30	Page 31
1.Who Am I? (pages 8&9) Habits Fears Patterns	2. Level of Consciousness	3. Manifestation	4. Who	5. Time	Emotional Gauge 6A. Negative Pages 22-25	for HHH Dowsing 6B. Positive Pages 26-28	7. Resolution	8. 100% Balance
Spirituality	Subconscious	Sensory Organ ears	Female - mother/her issue	About 15 years ago	Bereaved	Forgiving	Let it take care of itself. I write the issue out on paper	100%

Letting Go of Fear - Resolutions

Fear is what you have been creating and not what Heaven would give you.

Weaknesses
We can be trapped in them. Understanding them so we won't fall victim to them. Be thankful for the lessons learned.

You gain strength, courage and confidence by every experience in which you really stop to look fear in the face. You must do the thing which you think you cannot do.
Eleanor Roosevelt

LET GO of the things you no longer need, for example, clothes you have not worn for a year or so. This means detaching from material things, detaching from things which truly don't serve you any longer.   Attachments cause losses, attachments means having and making choices.

TEACH PEOPLE CORRECT PRINCIPLES, LET THEM DO THEIR WORK...
DO NOT BE ATTACHED TO THE OUTCOME.

IS IT YOUR EGO...MENTAL OR SPIRITUAL that is holding you back????
EGO is a survival tool but nothing beyond that...MASTER YOUR EGO...
ARE YOU IN CHARGE, OR THE EGO??? COMFORT ZONE IS AN EGO RUT.   BREAK IT.

The more you hate stuff, the more you intensify it, and give it your power. Judgment, hate comes always back to you. You must dive into the unknown...first a level of fear manifests: the EGO, WHICH IS THE PERSONAL SELF...YOUR LIFE MUST BE GIVING TO THE ULTIMATE BEING CONSCIOUSNESS.

FEAR AND JUDGMENT
By Craig.
Fear and judgment are based on fear. Do not judge anything. Do not give it good or bad meanings. The reality is that we are whole, complete, perfect and one. We have established the illusion that this is not so. We are often afraid of being who we really are. This fear is of ego alone. You create the illusion that you are afraid of either by making them yourself, or listening to the ratings of another person, that you value, above yourself. Examine all your past beliefs, you find these where often accepted without scrutiny. Now is the time to change all. ALWAYS examine your fears, you made them up or someone for you, you believe in them, you give them your power, this energy can be well used for other purposes.

MASTER YOUR FEAR...OR YOUR FEAR IS IN CHARGE OF YOU!

The Hardest Truth: In the end only one person in his world can drag you down or lift you up, and that person is YOU.

- THERE ARE NO VICTIMS-THERE ARE ONLY AGREEMENTS.
- IT IS GOOD TO EXPRESS...NOT REPRESS.
- STOP STRUGGLING...START STRIVING. DIVE INTO THE UNKNOWN.
- YOU CAN NOT INTIMIDATE ME ANY LONGER. GOD HAS GIVEN ME THE SPIRIT OF POWER, OF LOVE AND OF SOUND MIND...I FEAR NOTHING...LOVE CASTS OUT ALL FEAR ....

I am elevating my spirit to a higher consciousness (VIBRATION), where there is no illusions, NO FEAR, NO ANGER. There is only UNCONDITIONAL LOVE WITH GOD AND THE TOTAL UNIVERSE.

Habits are a comfort zone. Shift them as fast as you can, so you can grow. Break through this ENERGY. You find out how beautify every body is, everyone has a beautiful gift to give you, accept it with gratitude, love and feeling.

The impulse to wholeness is a natural birthright, for within each of us there is the possibility for wholeness and the deep desire to achieve it. Wholeness means being completely integrated, without any sense of being separated, fragmented or limited. It means experiencing real joy.

Boundless Energy
Deepak Chopra

#1 Who Am I - Core Pattern, Habits and Fears

Dowse through the following pages to learn what are my core patterns, habits and fears? Record on the <u>Issue Record Balance Sheet</u> (in appendix) Under Column #1 Who Am I?

#1A WHAT IS THE CORE PATTERN
If an issue shows up, please record go from 1 though 9 on the Issue Record Balance Sheet, #1
installed by others or my self?

PATTERN=repeating/understand them so you do not fall victim to them. Caught in a rut.

3year	Relationships
5 year	Marriages
7 year	Workplace, Careers
10 year	Diet, Health, Emotions, Mental attitudes,
etc.	Quitting try
	Behavior Pattern Character Flow
Addictions to sex, alcohol, drugs, food, people,	fault finder, mutineer, hero, caretaker, saver,
credit cards, doctors, belongings, antics.	adapter
Living in fantasy, Phobias, etc.	

Choice...Not change...Determines Destiny

#1B What are my
HABITS are our comfort zone, Break them.
If an issue shows up, please record go from 1 though 9 on the Issue Record Balance Sheet, #1
installed by others or by self

Feelings
1.   Self destruction - self denial - tired - sacrifice
2.   Calculator - drawnback
3.   Blaming - rebellion - dislike - shame - left out
4.   Resentment - compulsion - panic - respect
5.   Excusing - too busy - not enough time - involving
6.   Not enough energy - live too far
7.   Not protecting self - being a victim - surrendering - giving up power
8.   Self pity - misconception
9.   Avoidance - too much effort - worthlessness
10.   Running from or to, unwanted
11.   Playing games
12.   Being a rescuer - want to get rescued
13.   Jailer - prosecuting - judging - protesting - pretending
14.   Survival guilt - confrontation - risking
15.   Gossiping - being spontaneous
16.   Trapped - obligated - sorrow - sadness - frustrated
17.   Disappointed - dominant - difficult
18.   One-sided - competition - unwanted - unfairness
19.   Irritated - miserable - restlessness
20   Isolation - embarrassment - covering up - not setting   priorities - other's priorities
Dependency on Parents - Children - Partner - Government - work/boss
          Doctor - Caregiver - Friend - Phobias +/- etc.
Each civilization has a purpose, a lesson for that age
<u>Earth Cycles</u>
Repeating   1 week   2 weeks   3 weeks   4 weeks
Need to be selfless - help others to achieve their goal

#1C What are my
FEARS =   *F=False*
                 E=Evidence
                 A=Appearing
                 R=Real

                    Is the fear installed by others or by my self

What are your weaknesses?

Running away from fear.

Fear knocked at the door - when faith/truth answered no one was there.

To Conquer fear, we must face it.

1.   Fear of failure/success   School - Test - Teachers
         Fear used   as weapon - obedience/ rules - destructive emotion
2.   Making it on my own - survival
3.   Communication - commitment - new situation
4.   Losing identity - of God - Self
5.   Aging - loneliness - sickness - suffering - death
6.   Financial - Freedom -uncertainty
7.   Changes - Pressures - hassle - rejections
8.   To love - and being loved - deprived background
9.   Society - behavior - strangers- environment - danger
10.   Giving - receiving - trusting - believing - faith
11.   Future - past - present - accidents - limiting self
12.   Gaining weight - getting lighter in weight
13.   Working - boss - time - quitting - healing
14.   Heights - water - nature - thunderstorms - earthquakes - disasters - avalanches - tidewaters-tidal wave
15.   Insects - animals
16.   Crowds - open, closed spaces
17.   Ego - survival - environment - accidents
18.   Dependency on Parents - Children - Partner - Government - work/boss - Doctor - Caregiver - Friend
19.   Depend on you
20.   Blaming - uncertainty - emptiness - resentment
21.   Not being protected by family - God - Doctors, - Dentist - Hospital - Medication - Clinics Boss
         Hard road ahead
22.   Out of control - Missing something - worthlessness - Not having - Inadequacy, vulnerability, impatience

Check the level of consciousness.

When worry we loose our power within us.

If an issue shows up, please record in Columns 1 though 9 on the Issue Record Balance Sheet.

F=Frustration, hopelessness, futility	S=Sense of Direction
A=Aggressiveness (misdirected)	U=Understanding
I=Insecurity	C=Courage
L=Loneliness (Lack of oneness)	C=Charity
U=Uncertainty	E=Esteem
R=Resentment (Failure mechanism)	S=Self Confidence
E=Emptiness	S=Self Acceptance
	by Maxwell Multa, M.D. - Psycho Cybernetics

Spiritual/material Ego = Disease/Dis-ease of the spiritual ego
Need for love, security, creative expression, recognition, new experiences, self esteem

Dwell on the good things in your life
Parents - friends - brothers - sisters - relatives - neighbors - government
People we work with etc., bless them for they are our teachers
If you wait until you're completely ready or perfect, it usually is too late.

Please record anything that came up in response to the question "What are my Fears" on the <u>Issue Record Balance Sheet</u> under #1 Who Am I.

#2 Level of Consciousness
Column #2

Locate Point

Gain permission on all levels of consciousness

Level of Imbalance

Issues may often not be on a person's conscious level - things that happened during childhood or during times of stress may not be consciously remembered or recognized. Also people often have a Choice or No Choice in regards to an issue being put upon them. Sometimes what another person feels about you may affect you without you being conscious of it.

Thoughts have energy. If you have resistance on any level (Conscious, Subconscious, Superconscious, Unconscious, DUPI or Soul Conscious) in regard to our healing, your process will not move forward.

Conscious mind - we think with it all day long

Subconscious stores up memories

Superconscious - very powerful. We don't know much about it yet

Spiritual gifts and talent

All gifts - God's spiritual

Gifts must be used to help others positively

Do not waste time and energy trying to resolve all issues at once.

On What level of Consciousness is this issue showing up?

Conscious,	Subconscious,	Superconscious,	Unconscious, DUPI	Soul Conscious
	Chosen		Not Chosen	

Don't Judge - accept what Body, Mind, Spirit gives us (Eternal Being says.) Don't assume.

Please record on the Issue Record Balance Sheet, #2

18

#3 *How is the Issue Manifested on/in/around Body*

1. **Basic Unit** - Cell System

2. **Central and Peripheral Nervous System**

3. **Sensory Organs** (eyes, ears, nose, mouth, skin)

4. **Glands** - *internal secretion* (Endocrine - ductless) pineal, pituitary, thymus, thyroid, parathyroid, gonads (Male - testes, female - ovaries), adrenal - all secrete types of hormones
   external secretion (Exocrine - duct) liver, pancreas, sweat gland, gall bladder, salivary gland.

5. **Circulatory System** (Heart, vein, artery, capillary, blood)

6. **Digestive System** (mouth - teeth, gum, tongue, esophagus, stomach, duodenum, small intestine, large intestine, rectum)

7. **Reproductive System** (Male-penis, prostrate, scrotum, testes, etc.) (Female - breast, ovary, uterus, cervix, vagina, vulva, Fallopian tubes, etc.)

8. **Urinary Tract System** (Kidney, bladder, urethra)

9. **Structural System** (Skeleton, muscle, ligaments, tendons, etc.)

10. **Respiratory System** (nose, throat, trachea, lungs, bronchial tubes, air sacs, etc.)

11. **Immune System** (Lymph glands and nodes, tonsils, immune cells, adenoids, white blood cells, etc..)

12. **Chakra/Meridians** (Root-Crown Chakra)

13. **Subtle Body Layer** (See body Chart)

14. **Other Body components**

For other possibilities check anatomy books, physician's references, alternative healing approaches, etc...
Please record in Column #3 on the Issue Record Balance Sheet

#4 Who Caused this Issue?

Is this **MY or CLIENT** issue   **SOMEONE ELSE'S** issue
                                          BOTH of their Issues

male and female   male   female self group spirit

male/male   female/female alive   dead family thought form

solar   planetary world USA Native American   unknown

Please record on the Issue Record Balance Sheet, Column #4

#5 When did this issue arise?

Time period in which the issue came about or Time of Best Understanding of Issue's Origin:
Approximate time - Is it more than one year ago?
Less than one year ago (11 mo., 10 mo., etc.)?
1. past present   future
2. hour day   week month year ago/to come
3. past life   present life future life   parallel life
4. physical life times   how many incarnations ago   generations ago
5. in between lives during conception, after conception, during birth, after birth

Please record on the Issue Record Balance Sheet, Column #5

#6 Emotional Gauge
Please record on the Issue Record Balance Sheet, Column #6A & 6B

Refer to the Emotional Gauges on the following pages (or list pages if not here) to find the positive and negative feelings to help with the balancing of the issue. This is the most important feature in balancing or letting go of an issue or imbalance.

Emotional Gauge for HHH Dowsing
(dowsed and designed by A. Hagemann)

Find the most important Energy
which needs to be affirmed, embraced
with this Issue.

Find the most important Energy
which needs to be affirmed, embraced
with this Issue

Positive	*Neo Brain*	Negative
	above Crown Chakra	

Positive

Neo Brain
above Crown Chakra
transparent
Clearing
8

Negative

Determination , Truth
Expect Hugging Wholeness
Onward Provide
Wish Seeking

Cast out Irritated
Frames Inferior Lazy
(Too) Outspoken To speak out/up
Inability to speak

Assurance Absolute
At-one-ment Bliss
Brand New Correct
Expecting Erect
Encouraged
Involved Perfect

Crown
White
Appreciation
7

Behind Confused Loses
Encircled Fuming
Pointed Ruined
Not Listened to
Tight Too Young
Surprised Pride

Aware Buoyancy
Comparable Pride
Erect Determination
In Tune Relief

Brow
Indigo
Admiration
6

Encumbered Mean
Left Out Tight Young
Faded Resolved
Vulgar Unselfish
Troubled

Assurance Abstain
Beautiful Best Change
Enjoy Fulfilled Involved
Moving Precious Sign
Simple Turn To speak out/up

Throat
blue
Willing
5

Bold Challenged
Directed Evoked
Forgetting Hustled
Loveless Morbid
Not Generous Tempted
Outspoken Oppressed
Transgressed Infringed

Compassion Abstain Loving
Accommodate Clearing
Youngster Buoyancy
Compassionate Attainment
Divine Determination Expect
Moving Perfect Precise
Support Writing

Heart
Green
Attunement
4

Abject Yanking Stinky
Rigid Rotted Queer
Possessed Persecuted
Morbid Emptiness
Embarrassed Introverted
Hitched Grumbling
Youngster Immaturity

Attuned Adjusted Erect
In Tune Channel
Changeable Slender
Decision Employ Engaging
Accomplish Coexist Turn
Enchantment Loving Place

Solar Plexus
Yellow
Assurance
3

Antagonism Bribed
Paralyzed Confused
Defeated Evoked
Frightened Frustrated
Depressed

Acceptance Attuned Acquit
Climbing Collected Clearing
Delightful Elated Enfold Godly
Surprise Frugal
Knowing Myself In Time
Precious Wonder Transition

Sex
Orange
Interest
2

Conquered Depressed Zoned
Entangled Frightened Fuming
Indifferent Seeking Reform
Loaded down Void
Overreact

Choosing Changeable Dynamic
Employ Enfold Encouragement
Godly Knowing Lord Peace
Place Stability Trust
Onement

Root
Red
Oneness
1

Rejected Sorry for self Troubled
Trapped Humiliated Conceited
Lied About or To Oversensitive
Bereaved Overcharged Silent

EMOTIONAL ISSUES
Find the most important Energy which needs to be cleared (let go) with the issue.
Record in Column #6A
"Fear in your mind produces Fear in your life in Body-Mind-Spirit. This is the meaning of Hell!

You live on <u>borrowed</u> *or* <u>chosen</u> *emotions at times.*
Neglect   Accident   Shock   Trauma   Dis-ease
Source: Self   Other(s)   Situation

This may be how Body-Mind-Spirit feels.

1	2	3	4	5
Abuse (Emotional, Physical, Mental, Sexual, Spiritual)				
Anxiety	Anger	Assured	At fault	Agitated
Anxious	Affectionate	Annoyed	Attacked	Abandoned
Abasement	Abashment	Aback	Abatement	Antagonism
Abdication	Abduction	Abet	Abeyance	Abhorrent
Abiding	Abject	Able	Abnormal	Abolished
Abomination	Abortive	Aboriginal	Abrupt	Accountable
Accursed	Accusing	Acrid	Adventurous	
Boredom	Bothered	Burdened	Belligerent	Bitter
Betrayed	Bad-loscr	Bold	Backstabbing(ed)	Bad
Balking	Batter(ed-ing)	Bearing	Beaten	Begrudge
Beyond	Beguiled	Behind	Bereaved	Beseeched
Bewildered	Bypasses	Bribed		
Conflict	Crouching	Cynicism	Creative	Clinging
Cautious	Calm	Conceited	Compulsive	Conquered
Confused	Capricious	Captured	Cross	Critical
Cast out	Castaway	Caught	Cheap	Challenged
Cheated	Choked	Cluttered	Concerned	Confrontation
Conspiring	Contemptible	Countless	Costly	Crazed/Crazy
Disappointed	Depressed	Discontented	Distressed	Discontent
Disunited	Doubt	Directed	Dread	Discouraged
Dominant	Dominated	Diligent	Distracted	Dishonest
Disloyal	Dumb (mute or unintelligent)		Deprived	Defeated
Destructive	Disconnected	Disharmony	Disciplined	Deserted
Dead-end	Dislike(d)	Decrepit	Detailed	Disguised
Delude	Delusion	Demand	Detach	Disable
Envy	Exhausted	Exasperated	Empathy	Esoteric
Evocative	Evoked	Eye-for-detail	Eye-for-eye	Egotistical
Egoless/Ego	Egocentric	Embarrassed	Eliminated	Eluding
Embittered	Emptiness	Encircled	Encountered	Encumbered
Endangered	Endowed	Enslaved	Entangled	Enticed
Erased	Erratic			
Fear	Futile	Forlorn	Frustrated	Forgiving
Forgiven	Forgetting	Free(ing)	Fair	Fussv
Furious	Fuming	Fiery	Frightened	Friction
Frigid	Foul	Formidable	Faded	Fused
Festering	Fickle	Framed	Filthy	Fundamentalist
Facetious	Failure	Feeble	Fixed	Forceful
Forcible				

1	2	3	4	5
Guilt	Gut-feeling	Gaudy	Ghastly	Grouchy
Goaded	Gawking	Grudge	Giddv	Gimmicky
Gossipy	Greedy	Grievance	Grumbling	Gripping
Griping	Grief (for others/for self)			
Hurt	Hate	Humiliation	Helpless	Haughty
Humorless	Humorous	Hysterical	Hostile	Holding on
Hindered	Hoax	Hard	Hopeless	Harmful
Haunted	Heckled	Heaviness	Hesitant	Hitched
Horrible	Hurried	Hustled		
Intolerant	Impatient	Irritated	Irritant	Inner-direction
Inert	Insensitive	Imaginative	Impulsive	Irresistible
Individualistic	Injustice	Indignant	Intercepted	Indifferent
Ignored	Incensed	Immobilized	Inadequate	Insecure
Introverted	Inflated ego	interior	Inexpressible	Ineffective
Indulged	Intruded upon	Inebriated	Inconvenienced	Ineligible
Intelligent	Immaterial	Indomitable		
Jealous	Jammed	Justified	Justice	Jumpy
Joking	Jeopardized			
Know-it-all	Kinship	Knotted	Knocked-down	Knifed
Knowledgeable	Kind			
Lonely	Loaded down	Lonely	Lied to	Lied about
Lied for	Left out	Live in Fantasy	Loser	Lazy
Living in past	Lower	Limited	Lifeless	Listless
Least	Less	Liable	Let Down	Loss
Lost	Loveless	Lack of	Lassitude	Leaving
Load (Too heavy, big, small)				
Misfit	Miserly	Mistrust	Misconduct	Misbelief
Mad (Angry. Crazy)	Marked	Martyr	Mangled	Masked
Mean	Miser	Miserable	Morbid	Minced
Mindless	Misunderstood	Misunderstanding	Misjudged	Materialistic
Moody	Melancholy	Meticulous	Merciless	Misappreciated
Misappropriated				
Nervous	Not Understood	No Love (for/from, self, others)		Not happv
Not liked	Not listening	Not Listened to	Neglected	Noxious
Nonmaterialistic	Noisy	No faith in future	Numb	Not heard
No end	Not functioning	Not generous	Nonexistence	
Not taken (taking)care of	Not liking self/others			

Emotional Issues (cont)

1	2	3	4	5
Overloaded	Overburdened	Overworked	Over tired	Out of tune
Out of Balance	Orgasmic	Oversensitive	Offended	Overwrought
Outraged	Overwhelmed	Overweight	Overreact	Overact
Overtake/en	Opposing	Overlooked	Overcharged	Obstructed
Obnoxious	Odd	Off	Oppressed	Obsession
Outspoken				
Pain	Proud	Pathetic	Playful	Put oil
Put off	Pitiful	Picked on	Punished	Pessimistic
Paralyzed	Pointed	Prevailing	Prevailed upon	Picky
Polluted/rr	Possessive	Possessed	Passed	Prohibited
Parting	Progressive	Prosecuted	Persecuted	Pitied
Pity	Peculiar	Put down	Pursued	Put upon
Pretending	Panic	Psychic	Perverted	Pugnacious
Petrified	Perturbed	Patrolled/ing	Powerful/less	Permissive
Patronizing/ed	Plagued	Present	Putrid	Plain
Political	Promised	Provincial	Prevented/ive	Poisoned
Preserved/ing	Pressing	Pressed upon	Positive	Poised
Provocative	Procrastinate			
Questioned	Questioning	Quaking	Quarrelsome	Queasy
Queer	Quenched	Querying	Quip	Quitter
Quitting	Quiet	Quandary (in a)		
Released	Releasing	Retribution	Resentful	Realistic
Reclusive	Religious	Restless	Rigid	Repetitious
Resolved	Restrained	Rationalist	Rejected	Ruined
Recurring	Resentful	Resented	Reconverted	Reproached
Rage	Resigned	Racial	Rotted	Rebuffed
Reposed	Reflective	Reflecting	Reclining	Rude
Rudimentary	Repentant	Revenge	Reflecting	Reclining
Reckless	Resentment	Rough	Reproachment	Rut
Reaping				
Separation	Sarcastic	Seething	Sentimental	Self-pity
Shy	Sorry for self/others	See-no-end	See-not	Stubborn
Speechless	Soothing	Stressed	Stinky	Stingy
Spiteful	Sacrificing	Squandering	Self-punishment	Sorrow/for self/others
Sitter	Sitting,-out	Speak out	Self-esteem	Self-worth
Self-love	Sympathetic	Spontaneous	Strong-willed	Stagnant
Silly	Stupid	Suffering	Suffragette	Sober
Sensitive	Seeing	Seeking	Searching	Self-effacing
Sordid	Surfacing,	Sorting	Sullen	Self-empowered
Sticky	Situational	Suitable	Stuck-up	Screaming
Squelched	Smothering	Smothered	Smiling,	Soaring
Stuttering	Stirring	Strong	Satisfied	Saturated
Sad	Sassy	Skinny	Spongy	Symbolic
Struggling	Self centered			

Emotional Issues (cont)

1	2	3	4	5
Talented	Timid	Terror	Trustworthy	Tattle-tale
Thrifty	Thoughtless	Trapped	Threatened	Troubled
Trusting,	Trusty	Tortured	Taken	Tantrum
Tenacious	Thorough	Thrilled	Thrown away	Tight
Toxic	Tragic	Transgressor	Tricked/y	Turned in/ upon
Tough	Through	Thin	Thoughtful	Tribulation
Tempted	Transgressed	Teaching	Taught	
Used	Unreliable	Unaccepted	Unsubmissive	Ungiving
Unforgiving	Unfulfilled	Unappreciated	Uncourageous	Unresponsive
Uneasy	Unwelcome	Unhappy	Uncooperative	Unsolvable
Unlovable	Unloved	Uncontrollable	Undesirable	Unorthodox
Uneducated	Unrealistic	Unconventional	Uncontrollable	Unfair
Unacceptable	Unfulfilling	Uncaring	Unimportant	Unsupportive
Unengaged	Unwilling	Unsympathetic	Underage	Unseen
Unheard	Utilizing	Urged	Unstable	Underlined
Undertaken	Unknown	Unafraid	Unusual	Useless
Unnoticed	Unforeseen	Undeserving	Untold	Unfolding
Unforgiven	Unreadable	Undernourished	Undetermined	Underfed
Usable	Using	Underestimates self		
Vindictive	Vague	Vain	Voluptuous	Vengeance
Venture	Vicious	Villain	Vindicated	Vindicating
Violent	Virulent	Violated/ing	Vulgar	Voracious
Void	Valueless			
X-rated	Xenobiotic	Xenogeneic	Xenophobic	Xerophilous
Yapping	Yearning	Yelling	Yelping	Yabbering
Yacking	Yammering	Yanking	Yawning	Yawping
Yen	Yes-man	Yech	Yielding	Yodeling
Yogic	Yoked	Yoo-hoo	Yore	Young
Younger/est	Youngster	Yourself	Youth	Yowling
Yucky	Yuppie			
Zealous	Zero	Zealot	Zany	Zapped
Zonked	Zombie	Zoned		

See Other Issues Including those below:

Physical causes   Pathological causes   Physiological causes
Trauma causes   Mental/intellectual causes Relationship/social/family causes
Educational causes   Sexual Causes   Need to perform tasks

See **Emotional Gauge for HHH Dowsing**

See--counselor, psychiatrist, psychologist, 12 step programs

Exercise and other physical activities ---- action --- pinching, punching, running, walking, pillow fighting, running away or confronting others

Voice--crying, screaming singing, talking, listening

Creativity--drawing, painting, writing, reading

Check for-- lack of sleep, food, nutrition Chemical Causes

Check through Appropriate Books and Literature

Find the most important Energy which needs to be affirmed (embraced) with the issue.

Record in Column 6B

POSITIVE WORDS, STATEMENTS, FEELINGS
(This is how your Body-Mind-Spirit wants to truly feel)

1	2	2	4	5
Abide	Active	Angelical	Abilty	Actual
Appease	Able	Adaptable	Appreciated	Approachable
Artistic	Abound	Assured	Assurance	Attractive
Attuned	Available	Above	Add	At onement
At peace	Aware	Absolute	Adequate	Absolve
Adhere	Abstain	Adjust	Abundance	Admirable
Acceptance	Admissible	Adopt	Acclaim	Adorable
Accommodate	Adorn	Accompaniment	Adventurous	Accomplish
Affair	Affectionate	Accord	Afloat	Accredit
Aggrandize	Accrue	Aggrandize	Accurate	Alight
Align	Achieve	Alike	Alive	Allot
Acknowledgment	Acquaint	Acquire	Ambition	Acquit
Act	Amusement	Amused		
Balance	Beautiful	Become	Best	Blend
Bliss	Bold	Brand new	Busy	Buoyed
Buoyancy				
Called on	Calm	Caring	Celebrate	Certain
Challenge	Change/edd	Changeable	Channel	Choosing
Circulating	Clearing	Climbing	Coexist	Cognition
Cognizable	Collaborate	Collected	Comfortable	Complete
Committed	Communicate	Compassion	Comparable	Compatible
Compensate	Complete	Compliment	Compose	Comradery
Conceptualizing	Concerned	Connected	Considered	Consistent
Consolidate	Constancy	Consultative	Content	Contribute
Convenience	Conventional	Conversant	Cooperative	Cope
Correct	Creative	Constructive	Confident	Cheerful
Confrontation				
Daring	Decide	Decision	Delightful	Dependable
Deserving	Determination	Different	Divine	Dynamic
Dignified	Diplomatic			
Efficient	Elated	Elevated-	Emerging	Employ
Empower	Enchantment	Encouragement	Endeavor	Endurance
Enfold	Engaging	Enhance	Enjoy	Enlighten
Enter	Enthusiasm	Equal	Erect	Essential
Esteem	Eternal	Ever	Excel	Excepting
Excited	Expect	Extravagant		
Fabulous	Faith	Fantastic	Fidelity	Flexibility
Flourish	Forgo	Forthcoming	Fortunate	Forward
Frugal	Fulfilled	Future	Feel	Friendly
Frank	Firm			
Gentle	Giving	Godly	Gratuitous	Guided
Guidance	God Force	Generous		

1	2	3	4	5
Handling	Heal	Heartfelt	High	Honest
Hugging	Happy	Healthy	Harmonious	
Illuminated	Illustrating	Imperishable	Improving	In balance
Increase	Infinite	Innermost	Innocence	Innovation
Interested	In tune	Irradiant	Involved	Itself
Imagine	Integrity	Intelligence		
Jolly	Joy			
Kind	Kindly	Knowing	Known	
Leisure	Light	Lightened	Lord	Love
Lovely	Loving	Lyrical		
Manifest	Meditate	Mediate	Mellow	Mindful
Motivate	Moving	Myself	Mystic	
Needed	Negotiate	Nominal	Normal	
Observable	Oneness	Oneself	Onward	Open
Outreach	Overt	Optimistic	On time	
Parley	Passion	Peace	Perceptive	Perfect
Perseverance	Place	Play	Please	Pleasure
Pledge	Plentiful	Poise	Portray	Positive
Possibility	Practicable	Practice	Praise	Prayer
Precede	Precious	Prefer	Prepare	Prepossess
Presence	Present	Preserve	Prestige	Pride
Productive	Prosper	Protected	Proud	Provide
Purpose	Put	Patience	Promise	Principle
Persistent	Precise			
Quiet	Quick	Quoting		
Radiate	Radiant	Rate	Reach	Realm
Reason	Reassure	Receivable	Receptive	Reeducate
Reestablish	Refill	Refine	Reflect	Reform
Refresh	Regard	Rejoice	Relate	Relax
Release	Relevant	Relief	Relieve	Rely
Remark	Remind	Render	Replace	Replenish
Repose	Request	Require	Research	Reserve
Reunification	Review	Rise	Romance	Respect
Satisfactory	Select	Sensibility	Serve	Share
Sign	Signal	Simple	Sincere	Skillful
Slender	Smart	Sophisticated	Sound	Sovereign
Spontaneous	Stability	Stern	Strength	Suggest
Support	Surprise	Swept away	System	Speaking on/up
Self directed	Spiritual	Sensual		

1	2	3	4	5
Talent	Task	Team	Tender	Thanks
Tidy	Together	Total	Touch	Transform
Transition	Triumph	True	Trust	Turn
Twinkle	Truth			
Unify	Union	Unit	Unison	Universe
Unselfish	Unshaken	Up	Urge	Utter
Venture	Virtuous,	Vision		
Warrior	Willing	Welcome	Winning	Wish
Wonder	Writing	Wholeness	Won	
Yearn	Yield	Young		
Zeal	Zest	Zip		

This is what I wrote to my mother:
"MUTTI, you taught me strength, love, hugging. You did not control me, did not interfere in my life, always wanting the best for me. I am thanking you very much for everything painful and pleasurable. You were an inspiration for me. I always remember you. You are always in my life. Mutti, you also taught me fear of thunder and lightening which took me a long time to overcome. I now understand what brought it on by you and PAPI. thank you for the instilled fear. I finally let go of this fear which kept me from truly enjoying nature. After letting go by writing it out on paper, that day a tornado hit where I was staying and I never got out of bed.

This is what I wrote to my Dad:
"PAPI, You taught me honesty, heritage, strength, commitment to whatever I worked for, loyalty and more. I thank you for all you have done for me and with me. Through your illness and death you prepared me for my journey in my life. There was a lot of pain. I found out ..without pain, there is no gain in life. So thank you for everything I experienced with you. I love you. Your Anneliese.

Rolf ... sharing emotional, physical, mental, and unconditional LOVE with me, standing beside me in trying and good times, also thanking you for supporting me on my LIFE'S JOURNEY.

SELF ... choosing to change my attitudes, having faith in something higher than myself, to unconditionally love GOD, MYSELF and OTHERS, and respect myself and others in BODY, MIND, SPIRIT.

LETTING GO, writing out what does not serve you anymore is the best way to-let go of it from the physical, emotional mental, and spiritual (LEVEL) and from the conscious, sub-super-unconscious, DUPI and soul level of existence. If it is anger, hurt, pain, physical, mental, emotional sexual abuse, or whatever it is in your life which is holding you back of what you want to achieve .... like not being good enough, talked down to and all the feelings we store in us from parents, brothers, sisters, teachers or where ever these energies came from, LET THEM GO.......

LET THESE ENERGIES YOU ARE HOLDING ON TO **GO, GO, GO**.
IF YOU DONT LET THEM GO, THERE IS NO ROOM FOR NEW ADVENTURES TO COME IN YOUR LIFE

LOOK AT ME. I HAD TO OVERCOME A LOT TOO. I DID IT AND SO CAN YOU.
GET RID OF THE OLD (THE PAST)
MAKE ROOM FOR THE NEW (THE NOW).
THE PAST IS HISTORY.
THE FUTURE IS MYSTERY.
TODAY IS THE PRESENT AND A PRESENT TO YOU..
ENJOY THIS SPECIAL LIFE (GIFT) FROM GOD.

#7 Resolution - LET GO To balance

Are you willing to let go of the problem/Issue from all levels of consciousness and also from all parts of Body/Mind/Spirit/Soul?

1. Is it for the highest good of my client/self to write "The let go" out on paper?
2. To let go of all the issues at once
3. To think it out in their/my mind?
4. To scribble/draw/write on paper (person, thing)?
5. To write poetry.
6. To color/paint a picture.
7. To dance
8. To sing
9. To play an instrument.
10. To take a walk.
11. To play it out in a drama.
12. To shout/cry/scream it out.
13. To punch it out.
14. To talk to God.
15. To talk to the person/persons involved.
16. That my client and I go through it.
17. Thinking and breathing it out.
18. Hands-on to let go.
19. Is the educator to do it for the client?
20. Let it take care of itself.
21. To accept it as it is.
22. To allow the client to make their own decision.
23. Work with clay/sand/water/earth/garden etc.
24. Through recreation, sports (jumping rope, swimming, hiking)
25. Use crafts (knitting, crochet, sew, needle work)
26. Housework

This is my (our) issue (or this is not my(our) issue)? I let go of the (negative emotional vibration) which is held on my (whatever level of consciousness) and manifesting (in, on around my being). This energy vibration no long serves me. I now let it go for transmutation into healing energies and embrace the (positive) energy forever.
Thank you. Bless Love

or any other resolution.

#8 *Then dowse and ask if this problem/issue is 100% balanced.* If not, ask, "Do I need another negative/positive vibration to balance this Issue?", or use more BLESS LOVE to balance. Be sure you are always 100% balanced.

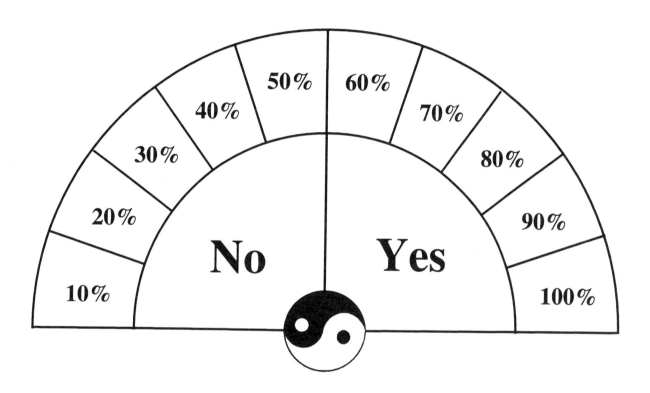

Beginning my New Journey =Living in my/God's Truth

1. What do these words mean? Goals, Dream, Desire, Vision, Mission.
Each person has a different concept of these words. Here are a few I searched out

Goals
Dreams
Desire
Emotions-Feelings
Vision
Life's Path
Mission

"Some people say they have not found themselves, but the Self is not something one finds. It is something one creates-uncovers."

Thomas Srass

"Your work is to discover your work(Life Mission) and then with all your Heart give yourself to it."

Buddha

Your true needs, wants, goals, desires, hopes, dreams, wishes and their fulfillment are as important as those of any other soul in existence.

I am not afraid of tomorrow for I have seen and experienced yesterday. And I love today, for today is the present, a gift to me from God. Thank you

It is the belief in a power larger than myself and other than myself, which allows me to venture into the unknown and even the unknowable.

Maya Angelou

Concepts, symbols, ideals, hunches, dreams, vision, intuition are all interpreted through our conscious mind. To receive it, is to believe it.

"Success usually comes to those who are too busy to be looking for it."
Henry David Thoreau.

Listen to your heart and knowing also that the work of self change is progressing in your Life. No regrets, only acceptance.

GOALS=Success, reaching a final purpose in life, scoring, end in life, the winning of a goal, a bound(?) where a journey is to end, an aim, ambition, finish line, point, marker, direction. Could be material things, like a home, automobile, a new dress, money in the bank, a vacation, a new relationship, climbing a mountain, being in a movie, Olympics, etc.

"The Journey to your Goal is more important than your goal - Focus on the Journey itself"
Success or failure is caused more by mental attitudes than by mental capability.

DREAMS=vision, fantasy, daydreams, imagination, exceptional gifts, divine message of approach. If there where dreams for sale, what would you buy? *"Listen to your heart and receive the understanding that you are deserving of your dream."*

Dreams do come true, if we only wish hard enough. You can have anything in your life, if you are willing to sacrifice everything else for it. "What will you have? says God. Pay for it and take it.
James Barrie.

The greater things.
Great it is to believe the dream.
When we stand in youth by the stream
But a greater thing is to fight life through and say on the end -"The dream was true."
Edwin Markham

DESIRE=is wanting, wishing, requesting
"Our driving tool is our desire. Are you hiding yours?"
We are not born uninterested. You are never given a wish without also being given the power to make it come true. You may have to work for it, however.

You are what your deep driving desire is.
As your desire is, so is your will.
As your will is, so is your deed.
As your deed is, so is your destiny.

Brahadaranyaka Upanishad

We are like a clock which has all the "Works" to make it run. Desire is the key that winds it. Love gives it the rhythm.

EMOTIONS=Feelings, great sensibility, act or condition. Passion, judgment, sympathy, romantic, joy, grief, fear, hate, love attitude, sensation of touch, sense, taste, smell, perception, a sense of being. Very little is needed to make a Happy Life. It is all within yourself, in your way of thinking.

I am changing things
I can see things happening
I talk about them, and I make them happen.

VISION=art of seeing (sight) with or without the eyes. A fancy view, visualizing your goal, mental image or picture To become the vision

Your life within Gods perfect plan - pay attention to what you know you are on Earth to do. You need a strong vision. The vision pulls you through difficulties in Life

To become the vision, you must surrender your greater Self (God) which means, you must take the Leap of Faith - Truth - Trust.

LIFE'S PATH=A Life Way, a course, track of life, way of passage, moving from one point to the other, progress, direction of goal route, career.
Live from the inside out, not from the outside in.

"Creating the Future begins with action taken in the Present"

"The Earth School Experience has been set up by you to learn the path of the heart."

MISSION=To send on, entrust with, delegating, duty you are sent on, messenger, a calling, a station of mission. army errand, task, assignment, commission, missionary work.

"Each soul enters with a mission. We all have a mission to perform."

"Open the doorway to your mission, open your heart and just listen"

Write down all the things you considered doing in you life. Which suits your nature. Is this a 10, 9, 8 for the next two years? Then dowse out what # it is. You want to shoot for a 10 or 9.
You Know #10 is for your Highest Good
#9 is Very Good
#8 is Good
#7 is OK - don't sell yourself short - Not enough energy here.

Things I'd Like to Do	Rating

What I am is God's Gift to me. What I make of myself is my Gift to God

Success from Dr. Robert Schuller

4 P's
1. **Purpose**
2. **Passion - Enthusiasm**
3. **Principles**
4. **Partnership (God/Truth)**

If you get to where you're going, where will it be?
What I be, is up to me

Yet it is not the past that reveals your direction, but the purpose with which you move.
The Third Millennium.

Ask yourself these questions and write them down:

1. ***Why did I get up this morning?***
Is it to eat, to work, to have fun, to help others to survive (money/job)?
Are you happy in your job, career, training? Successful people in general do what they really want to do in their lives.

Are you a fully grown bird, but afraid to fly away from the nest, to fly on your own journey?

Have your written a "Will for Living?" (Where are you going and how to get there.)

2. ***What are you looking for in a job-career-training*** ? Pay, hours, holidays, fringe benefits, automatic increased) or are you looking for a new exciting way of learning new skills, new knowledge, meeting interesting people and places?

If you are looking or a money making business, job and you do not like what you are doing, you are not going to make the money which you expect. When you like what you are doing, you make the money and more, you are happy, satisfied and at peace with yourself. Put service first and money takes care of itself.

3. ***Why was I born?***
You asked to be born, you chose your vehicle and potential experience. Under divine guidelines. What progress have you made since you came?

Your body is constantly revealing your purpose to you, are you listening?

When you feel you've wasted time, think of it as training for your Soul purpose.

When you are not happy with who you are, your Soul is talking to you. Are you listening?

We are masters of our Souls. What we think we attract.

Take a good honest look within, at your Emotion and your deepest beliefs and your ability to receive. They are the only obstacles to finding and living your bliss.

Create the canvas of your Life, your ♥ your Soul as you truly desire it to be.

If you don't plan a direction in life, you have made a choice, that of no choice.

What do you want to do in the future?
<u>Make short term personal and social goals</u>
<u>Long term personal goals</u>
<u>Professional goals</u>
What do you want to do three years from now
....six years from now?

If you answer these questions, you have no right to be disappointed when you are unhappy in your present situation.

If you have trouble establishing your Goals, look back upon your life. In retrospect what are the highlights? These can be good clues for the future. Fantasies are also good clues. Commit your goal to paper. Remembering that you can create any reality within the perspective of your background and potential experience, as long as it doesn't require manipulation of someone else. You simply have to be willing to pay the price. This could be time, effort, perseverance or risk.

I am elevating my Spirit to a higher consciousness (vibration), where there is no Illusion, no Fear, No hatred, no anger. There is only Unconditional Love with God and the Total Universe.

Are you a can, or a cannot?
Cans vs. Cannots
The polarization of America
Ask yourself, What am I doing it for?

Edgar Cayce stressed using Decency-order.
He suggested that we should not *"Put our Hands to the plow unless we are determined to follow through."*

Having a sound business plan with adequate funds to back this effort is very important.

Purposeful-meaningful activity
New ideas
New source
Brain power

<u>Define your goals</u>
<u>Work out definite program</u>
<u>Set up timetables</u>
<u>Concentrate on essentials</u>

Success or failure is caused more by mental attitudes, than by mental capability (repeated from earlier)
No one plans to fail - some just fail to plan/

Take chances. No man is worth his salt who is not ready at all times to risk his body, to risk his well-being, to risk his life for a great cause.

Theodore Roosevelt

Hell is Truth seen too late.

Adam

The force is within you. Force yourself.

The healthiest attitude is to realize that the unknown is just another term for "creation."

Deepak Chopra

Until one is committed

there is hesitancy. the chance to draw back,

always ineffectiveness.

Concerning all acts of initiative (and creation),

there is one elementary truth,

the ignorance of which kills countless ideas

and splendid plans:

that the moment one definitely commits oneself,

then Providence moves too.

All sorts of things occur to help one

that would never otherwise have occurred.

A whole stream of events issues from the decision.

raising in one's favor all manner

of unforseen incidents and meetings

and material assistance,

which no man could have dreamed

would have come his way.

I have learned a deep respect

for one of Goethe's couplets:

"Whatever you can do. or dream you can, begin it.

Boldness has genius, power. and magic in it."

From The Scottish <u>Himalayan Expedition</u>
by W. H. Murray
Published by J. M. Dent & Sons Ltd.. 1951

How to Be Rich and Happy *Internally*

1) Live your ideal life ... now!

2) Do things that are extraordinary and nearly impossible.

3) Believe that: If it is to be, it is up to me.

4) Think BIG! Dream lofty dreams. Plan. Act immediately.

5) Keep in contact with the best, meet people engaged in the best, experience the best.

6) Be your own boss: Do what you love and get paid for it.

7) Take self-inventory annually on your birthday.

8) Increase your income daily-whether you work, play, or sleep.

9) Do what you do so well that people enthusiastically refer others to you.

10) Inspire others by your example.

11) Build your reputation for honesty, integrity, quality, and super service.

12) Aim for excellence in your field.

13) Support others in achieving their goals.

14) Develop influential friendships worldwide.

15) Take total responsibility for your past, present, and future experiences.

16) Strive to accomplish more with less time, money, and energy.

17) Do not criticize, condemn, or complain.

18) Act as if it were impossible to fail.

19) Dine at the finest restaurants.

20) Dress to look and feel great! (Mostly solid colored clothing.)

21) Collect quotes that motivate you.

22) Speak and write only positive words.

23) Carry a crisp $100 bill with you at all times.

24) Learn something new every day.

25) Exercise at least 20 minutes daily to achieve and maintain your ideal body.

26) Do and say things that benefit all concerned.

27) Be open to new ideas, relationships, and experiences.

28). Realize that all events happen for the best.

29) Plan to do two significant things a year.

30) Build a personal-development library.

31) Take calculated risks to get ahead.

32) Read books by and about people you admire.

33) Simplify your life-live more fun per hour.

34) Know that you are equal to everyone and everyone is equal to you.

35) Accept people for the way they are and the way they are not.

36) Forgive and love everyone.

37) Do what you feel is best, no matter what people think of you.

38) Catch people "doing it right" and praise them.

39) Save 10% of your net income.

40) Give something away daily-a postcard, letter, gift, smile, hug, compliment.

41) Collect pictures of what you want to be, do, and have in life.

42) Eat mostly fresh fruits, vegetables, nuts, and grains.

43) Avoid saying *can't, hard, or difficult. Say I can, it's easy, and it's simple.*

44) Keep your home, desk, closets, clean, neat and organized.

45) Use a simple time-management system.

46) Listen to music that motivates you.

47) Spend more time with nature.

48) Act as if all your goals have already been achieved.

49) Take a winner to lunch.

50) Constantly escalate your goals.
(Thank you for the 50 positive statements. I found this without a name)

LIFE'S PATH - SOUL MISSION

Write it out and record on RECORD SHEET II on page 44.

Dowse out if everything has been fulfilled in your life at this time. This gives you some clues where you are going.

1. **Physical** - food, clothing, health, home, automobile, furniture, travel, hobbies, leisure, sports, etc.

2. **Mental, emotional, intellect** - education (schooling) emotional, self worth, acceptance, etc.

3   **Spiritual** - tools, resources, religious, spiritual education, etc.

4. **Education** - schooling, certificates, medals. (Education, mental, physical, emotional, nutritional, religious, spiritual),etc.

5. **Family** - Grandparents, parents, siblings, marriage, in-laws, children, grandchildren, etc.
    Spiritual, Children of the World

6. **Financial**, savings, real estate, business, investment, pension, etc.

7. **Relationships** - female/male, animals, public, friendships, etc.

8. **Sexual** - sacred, unity. etc.

9. **Social** - work, experience, occupation, career, self expression, organization, technology, culture, events, etc.

For info: Please check the book TO OUR HEALTH, Using the Inner Art of Dowsing in the Search for Health-Happiness-Harmony

LIFE'S PATH - SOUL MISSION
Write it out record on Page 44

1. Self Discovery - Who Am I?
    Finding my place and function in my Life's Mission.

2. What are my Goals, Dreams, Desires, Emotions, Vision , My life's Path, Soul Mission?

3. What did I achieve so far in my Life?

4. What do I want to achieve in my Life? spiritual/material - both?

"I must know what I am capable of, before I know where I am going with my Life's Path Soul Mission, lest I go nowhere at all."

5.	What are my abilities? -Natural or acquired? Things I already do? Knowledge of my aptitudes - where I excel is the most important factor in selecting my Path Mission. Learning styles? What is for my Highest Good? What is fulfilling and rewards me as I deserve?

6.	Am I capable of delegating, managing, negotiating, organizing, persuading, selling, supervising?

7.	Am I skilled in the Art of Reasoning, simplifying, involving problems, drawing solutions, conclusions, information?

8.	Am I able to help others, solve personal problems. Can I motivate others, advise, guide or counsel them? Nurturing.

9.	Am I capable of serving people on a spiritual level? Emotional and Physical level?

10.	What are my strengths? How Can I use them?

11.	Am I doing this for myself, God, World, others, parents, partner, children.

12.	What factors play an important role in my life?
	Is it marriage, children, parents, family, neighbors, sexuality, circle of friends, money, status, work, superiors, colleagues, hobbies, journeys, youth work, social assistance, health field, spirituality, etc. Material success, survival talents.

13.	What are my tools - wisdom, drive, focus, responsibilities, commitment, direction, planning, High self esteem, trustworthy uniqueness, unconditional love

14.	Do you strive or just survive?

15.	Is your Life Mission/Vision heart directed?

CH-CH-CH-Changes - Chances

Give yourself an extra month each year to reach your goals. Simply eliminate the false mindset of "not enough time". Get up an extra half-hour early or go to bed a half-hour later each night (When you exercise more, eat better, and have positive reinforcing thought you may find that you can do with a half hour less sleep.) Use that time to either work on your goals or on yourself. It may not be much time in and of itself, but it sure adds up. A half-hour extra, six days a week, is three hours a week. That's 166 extra hours or more than four forty-hour work weeks extra per year!

LIFE'S PATH SOUL MISSION

Balance is the key to wholeness.
Often the difference between a dream and a desire is simply getting it on paper.
<u>Write down</u> all the things you like to do and consider doing in your life what suits your soul.

Places to go

_____

People you want to know.

_____

Ways to change myself & the world

_____

Adventures/Cultures

_____

Books to read/to learn

_____

Crafts/sports I want to learn

_____

Religions, philosophies I want to study

_____

What did you like to do at different ages in your life

     1-10 years_____

     11-20 years_____

     21-30 years_____

     31-40 years_____

     41-50 years_____

     51-60 years_____

     beyond 61 years_____

Who do you like to be with (people)?

_____

Do you like to be alone, in a group with people, animals?

_____

What are your hobbies?

_____

Do you like to work(be of service) during the day or at night?

_____

Are you willing to reorganize your time?

_____

What are you willing to give up (time, money, being away from your family, friends, home, surroundings, country)?

_____

What are you willing to invest (time, money, Gifts you have)?

_____

Are you willing to go back to school (formal, informal, skill training)?

_____

Are you willing to change your occupation, take a lower paying job for you happiness?

_____

Are you willing to move to a different place?_____

Are you willing to commit drive, focus, be optimistic, put action behind it, go the distance, and
     be responsible._____

What are your responsibilities/commitments in your life at this time? What are the limits?

_____
_____
_____
_____

Define what do you really desire, want and dream of in your life.
You then set it into your subconscious mind and out to the Universe to manifest.

_____
_____
_____
_____

WRITE IT OUT ON PAPER VERY IMPORTANT!!!!!

FINDING YOUR LIFE'S PATH, YOUR SOUL MISSION

AWAKENING THE ME WITHIN Desire Goals Dreams Vision Interest Freedom Travel Choices Right Place Financial Freedom	People you want to be with	How much resources (i.e., time, money) do you want to give it	For whom? Self, family friends, world	Qualifications What skills, loves? Do I have these skills/interests?: managing negotiating supervising selling persuading organizing delegating guiding counseling Advising guiding counseling motivating nurturing serving drawing solutions simplifying information learning logic	To go back to school/change jobs	What do I gain? Creative expression, recognition new experiences Self esteem more life	Responsibilities Commitment Focus Direction Self esteem trust worthy uniqueness unconditional love	Activities	6th Sense Intuition Dowsing Gut feeling God Feeling

BUSINESS

(Occupations, professions, and possible positions and problems are listed below)
Suitable or right livelihood. (Are you creating negativity through your livelihood, i.e., dishonest, exploitative? Employment should not create paranoia and separateness in the World)

Business management   Marketing   Financing
Corporation   Corporate power   (CEO, Executives)
Accounting   Technological advice
Hospitality management   Applied computer technology
Engineering – mechanical   electrical   civil   industrial
Computer programming personal/business computer
Specialist – Computer - assisted bookkeeping PC repair
Desktop Publishing   Design Catering—Gourmet cooking cafeteria
Medical Office assistant   Dental Assistant
Auto mechanic   Drafting   Animal Care Specialist   Travel agent
Air-conditioning/heating and refrigeration   Secretary
Electrician   Police Science   Private Security Officer
Art - painting, drawing, sculpting   Small Business management
Legal Assistant   Interior Decorating   Wildlife/forestry
Conservation Gun Repair   Locksmith   Motor Cycle Repair
Surveying/Mapping   Fitness   Nutrition   TV/VCR Repair
Child Day Care Provider/Owner   Photography
Dressmaking/design   Journalism   Short story writing   Florist
Teacher's Aide   Home Inspector   Medical Transcriptionist
Real Estate Appraiser Appliance repair   Hotel/restaurant management
Tax Preparation   Crafts Farmer   Funeral Director   Fire Fighter
Pattern/model/papermaker
Assessor/controller/Treasurer   Police/Detective
Interviewer   Recreation   Construction/Carpenter
Dishwasher/Waitress Drywall Installer   Lather Punch Press Excavation   Brick mason
Stone mason   Roofer Slater Cement Finisher   Assembler Freight   Sales Photographer
Artist   Counselor   Doctor (many types)   Psychiatrist/Psychologist
Model Actress/actor
International/overseas Small business/large business

For the Highest good of Family/Children
Both member of family should work - mother/father
One parent needs to stay home for children

Not capable of organizing a business   Highly capable to organize and run a business
Should own and run own business   Should have partner/change partner
Be careful with choosing customers/partners   Relocate business   Close business
Advertising needed   change of advertising tactics
Add on to business   Streamline business
Use business to help community

Dowse out where your personality, character and work habits lie.

PERSONAL ANALYSIS AND POTENTIALS

PERSONALITY	CHARACTER	WORK HABITS
Artistic	Dignified	Adaptable
Creative	Abrupt	Variety and Change
Visionary	Critical	Attention to Detail
Changeable	Cheerful	Detail Work
Impulsive	Jealous	Routine Work
Responsive	Envious	Initiative
Reserved	Friendly	Memory for Names
Sympathetic	Frank	Memory for Faces
Resentment	patient	Memory for Details
Prejudice	Impatient	Memory Oral Instructions
Expression-Oral	Outspoken	Memory Written Instructions
Expression-Written	Imaginary	Work Alone
Decision	Extravagant	Work with Men
Logical	Generous	Work with Women
Investigative	Pessimistic	
Comprehensive	Optimistic	
Self-sacrificing	Moody	
Stability	Pride	
Adventurous	Spiritual	
Stubborness	Sensual	
Joiner	Show-off	
	Secretive	
Are you:	Vain	
	Benevolent	
	Domineering	
Introvert Extrovert	Deceitful	
(needs to be alone) (needs to be w/people)	Diplomatic	
Both	Cooperative	
	Constructive	
Thinking Type / Feeling Type	Integrity	
External laws Uniqueness in every	Keeps Promise	
principles in judging Situation	Good Principle	
Both	Loyal	
	Persistent	
Sensing Type Intuitive Type	Procrastinates	
tangible practical Creative, Imaginative	Self-Centered	
concentrating on	Self-Confidant	
here and now	Underestimates Self	
Both		

The Force (God) Spirit is within you.
That Force is there to find your desires, your growth (Development)

NOW PLAN

What do you want to be when you grow up? Making plans - go where you are called
A carpenter, a house engineer, a star, a beggar, a spiritual leader, etc. Desires - do the things you love Make a list of your desires, dreams, goals, vision Find your occupation, career, job, owning your own business.   Look in the back pages of this book and dowse what is for your/God's highest good and for the good of all

"Listen to your heart and know that the work of self change is progressing in your life."

Relax, remember this is something you are doing for your self (Soul, God)

Desire List

Short Term	1 month	1 year	5 years	10 years or more
Clean closet write to people read a book watch a movie make a phone call	Put $5.00 in your bank account Help others with food, etc.	Find a partner make a commitment buy a car travel have a family	buy a house retire early	Live in another country

You can create and have everything you choose, Work it and make it work for you.

Dowse through these pages for your Life's Path=Soul Mission Opportunities. Write them down. Then use the chart to determine what is in your highest good and the good of all.

Individuality, activity, decision making abilities
Leadership qualities, initiative and aggression
Opportunities Potential Self Empowerment

A Architect Army-Navy-Air Force
  Ambassador Airlines (work with) Author
  Actor Administrator Amusement
  Advertising Analyst Artist Archaeologist
  Antique Dealer Attorney Arbitrator Art
  Gallery Accountant Automobile Dealer -
  Service Astrologer Agriculture
  Anthropologist Architect Animal Shelter
  Animal Care

B Businessman/woman Business Commerce
  Buyer Bookkeeping Brain Surgeon
  Bellboy Baker Banking Industry - Teller,
  Management Beautician-hair expert
  Barber Bridgebuilder Butcher Biologist
  Basketball, Baseball player Biographer
  Bricklayer Big Game Hunter Broker Bus
  transport

C Creative Artist Crafts Chemist
  Consumer's Rights Cabdriver City Guide
  Clairvoyant Character analyst
  Construction (lumberyard) Clairaudient
  Car Dealer Car Sales Cashier Card Reader
  (tea leaf)

D Dance instructor Departmental head
  Drug related Doctor of [Medicine
  Chiropractic Osteopathy Naturopathy]
  Dentist Dental assistant Dental laboratory
  Dietitian Driving instructor Detective
  Dealer/car/care, etc. Draftsman Detail
  Work Dry-cleaning, Dramatic art

E Editor Exterminator Explorer Entrepreneur
  Efficiency Expert Economist Entertainer
  Electrician Engineer Engraver Educational
  Service

F Fashion designer Film (Actor, Director,
  Production) Food caterer/management
  Football . (coach, player, management)
  Farmer (agriculture) Factory Forestry
  Furniture maker Finance Florist

G Garage mechanic Guidance Counselor
  Gynecologist Government related work
  Gospel singer Game inventor Gymnast
  Gardener Grocery manager Grave digger
  Grave stone maker Gambler

H Hotel manager Handwriting expert Hostess
  Horticulturist House painter Humorist
  Hospital Housewife Health care Service
  Healer Healing arts Historian Hypnotist

I Illustrator Inspector Inventor Ice hockey
  (player, scout, management) Insurance
  Interior decorator Investigator Investor

J Jeweler Journalist Judge Janitor

K

L Lawyer Librarian Linguist Lecturer
  Landscaper Leader Law enforcement
  Legal service

M Movie maker marriage counselor mountaineer mystic manufacturer museum mayor mushroom grower mediator minerals magician music related musician medical doctor mason minister miner missionary mathematician manager model military

N Numerologist Nurse Novelty maker Newspaperman Navigator Novelist Natural science Nature

O Organizer, Office, Oceanographer, Occult Expert, Oil Related

P Parish Priest Policeman, Philanthropist Pawnshop owner Philosopher Poet Physicist Psychologist Physicist President Psychic Personnel Management Prime Minister Painter Parachute Politician Photographer Palmist Pilot Public Relations Psychiatrist Publishing (agent, house) Professor Plumber Promoter Pharmacologist Proof reader Professional Athlete Printer Publicity Agent Psycho-analyst Police work Performing arts

R Reporter Real Estate Agent Research work Rock and Roll group Roadworks Researcher Racing (car etc.) Revolutionary Radio Retail Religions Railroad Recreation

S School-College Principal Sky diver Sportsman Sports instruction Secretary Speculator Surgeon Statistician Seer Sea Captain Social Work Field Social Director Social Service Spy Secret Agent Spiritual Medium Student Scientist Singer Statesman Seamstress Salesman Director Salesman Saleswoman Stone Worker Speech Writer Short Order Cook Sculptor Science - medical, electrical mechanical Special Trade Sanitary Space travel

T Teacher Travel Guide Television show host Time motion studies expert Timetable Schedules Town planner Trader Toy manufacturer Tutor Tennis Player Tailor Theatrical Travel Connected Transportation

U Undertaker Union leader

V Veterinarian Volunteer

W Writer, Window decorator Waiter/waitress Wood related Wholesales

Envision your true/Truth Life's Path Journey
Planning, Making your Desire-Dream Vision Creation

Look through catalogs, magazines. Use pictures, postcards, symbols, nature, use whatever your Soul-Heart desires. Glue, write, paint, draw, sketch, model your canvas/map of Enlightenment. Whatever you create, you believe you receive

This is my Life's Path and Soul Mission Canvas

My Soul mission is living and working in God's truth, be an example to mankind, and share with others how they can heal themselves

Mission statement: I am a spokesperson for the Truth. I feel peaceful, joyful, healthy, happy and in harmony. I love Life and everything that goes with it. I live in God's Bliss.

"Each soul enters with a mission. We all have a mission to perform."

Say YES to yourself
I can do it. I am motivated. I am inspired
I have confidence. I can manage my self.
I have help from above and around. I have the power of accepting and expecting.
You only need to ask for guidance
You have to have total Belief (in yourself)
Total Trust in something higher than yourself.
Know the Truth, Total Faith in God and yourself

To relinquish total control is my spiritual goal. Totally Free - living in simplicity, strength, stamina in my/God's Bliss-Health-Happiness-Harmony.

Guidelines
Make yourself worth knowing!
keep alive and growing
Plan regular development of your mind and interests!
Present yourself attractively!
create the impression you want
Build a reputation which attract people!
Show your respect to other people!

May God, Great Spirit "Bless You," protect you, and show you the way to your Highest Truth. Move forward, follow your/God's Truth and vision. Bless Love.
Anneliese

We deserve to be prosperous and to enjoy our work, accepting money as a way of loving ourselves enough to buy the experience in life we deserve. Good works shall gain you honor in the market place.

Divine Truth
The fruit of the True Spirit
Love, Joy, Peace, Patience, Truth and Kindness

Going the Distance

The will to go the distance is the key to any goal;
To stick it out despite the odds, to choose the winner's role,
Or it would be so easy not to make a choice at all;
To turn your head the other way and just ignore the call.

One choice leads to a mountain - the other to a bog.
One leads up where the air is pure - the other through a fog.
To choose the right is surely hard, its challenges are tough.
Its climb is steep and awesome; its surfaces are rough.

The multitudes just drift along with false pride in their voice.
And spend their days in vain pursuit of meaning in their choice.
Tho they could find fulfillment, and they could feel the touch
Of goals and growth and greatness - that just requires "too much".

But you decide to leave the crowd and take the upward way,
To seek a goal, to pay the price, despite what others say;
You make your own commitments - it's your grit that pulls you through,
So if you can't believe it - just pretend that it is true.

A small glimpse of your winning might be all that you would need.
At times it seems so far away you think you can't succeed.
The distance is not measured in what you have done before
What lies ahead you cannot see - it may not be much more.

And at the top, a fantasy of all that you could dream
A rainbow of your happiness and joy a constant stream
Then looking out from lofty heights of where you're running free
You see the path to greatness in your own reality.

When you reach your goals and you look back on what you've feared,
You find it much more beautiful than upward it appeared.
So if you go the distance it won't matter how you came,
With doubt and fear or speed and joy you get there just the same.
GO THE DISTANCE

H.M. Risinger

Optimism

What difference does it make if we see a
glass as half-full or half-empty?
In both cases, the water level is exactly
midway between the top and bottom.
So what do you gain by seeing the glass as
half-full? You begin to believe that it will become
even more full. You see the world in a more
positive light, and put your mind at ease.
You begin to have faith that your side
will win...that you can achieve what you want
to achieve. That's good. Just make sure that
you don't see the glass as half-full when it's
really only one-tenth full!

Rick Bayan

Commitment

Our language is full of delightful oddities.
When you pursue a long-term goal, we say
you're committed. But we use the same word
to describe someone who's been forced to
enter a mental institution!
Maybe that's not so odd after all. You see,
every commitment forces you to surrender
some of your freedom. If you decide to become
an architect, then you can't be a brain surgeon.
If you marry Pat, you can't marry Chris.
That's what makes commitment so scary.
But take a hard look at the alternative:
living in a state of perpetual indecision,
waiting in vain for your life to begin.
Test the waters! Take the plunge.

Rick Bayan

Focus

Most of us have at least a vague idea of what
we want tot accomplish in life. But a vague idea
is like a snapshot that's out of focus.
You can see what's in the picture - but
everything's blurred and hazy.
It's like saying, "I want to be a writer."
That's a brave ambition, but it's not in focus.
Would you write fiction? Nonfiction?
Drama? Poetry? Journalism?
What kind of audience would you write for?
What education will you need?
Whenever you come up with an idea,
keep focusing until your mental picture
is sharp and filled with details.
Then develop it!

Rick Bayan

Where to look for Self Change Opportunities

* People you know -
* Direct employer contact
* Newspaper want-ads
* Job Service
* Private employment agencies
* Yellow pages
* School placement offices
* Libraries
* Government listings
* Newspaper articles
* Spiritual Centers/Churches
* Health Centers
* Bookstores
* Volunteering

* Television/radio
* Entrepreneurship
* (Wisconsin) Career Information System
* Bulletin boards
* Union halls
* New business construction
* Chamber of Commerce
* Help-wanted signs
* Professional and trade associations
* Internet
* Holistic Clinics
* Complementary Medicine
* Hospitals/Clinics, Drugstore

Volunteering is a health habit because it

* **brings** satisfaction **helping** others
* Promotes camaraderie
* imparts knowledge
* is self-rewarding
* encourages teamwork
* stimulates **the** mind
* helps **the community**
* allows one to serve another
* develops **new** friendships gets
* provides new opportunities for learning

* broadens experiences
* utilizes skills and talents
* creates a sense of well-being
* is stress-relieving
* keeps one active and involved
* brings joy to others
* gives one a purpose
* keeps you young
* gets you out of **the house!**

Private Employment Agencies

Employment agencies are businesses that attempt to match job seekers with jobs. As a business, they must charge either the employer or the job seeker for their service. Look for employment agencies that specialize in your specific occupation.

Temporary employment agencies place people in temporary positions for varying lengths of time. When placed, you are actually an employee of the agency rather than an employee of the place you work. Some employers "try out" employees as "temps" and buy out the contracts of "temps" they like, at which time you become an employee of the company, not the agency. Temporary employment may be a way of getting your "foot in the door" or trying out new jobs.

Yellow Pages

The telephone Yellow Pages are an excellent resource for putting together a list of potential employers. itprovidesbasicinformationaboutemployers-thebusiness'name,addressand telephone number- Use the index of the Yellow Pages to identify categories of employers that might be interested in a person with your skills. Write down these categories and then look within each category to develop your list of individual employers to contact directly.

School Placement Offices

Most public and private schools have a school placement office to help individuals find work. These

offices may only assist current students or alumni of the school or occasionally the general public. Contact placement offices to find out if they can help you.

Libraries

Libraries have countless materials available to you - materials that will help you discover hidden job leads. Telephone directories, newspapers, business directories, professional and trade journals, company databases and annual reports are few of the materials you might find helpful. Many libraries have typewriters, computers and photocopiers available to the public for little or no charge. They also have books, videos and audiocassettes available for loan on job hunting, job interviewing, resume writing, careers and employment testing.

Government Job Listings

Federal,state,county,city,village and town hiring unita earch lis their own job openings. Use your telephone book to locate the government agencies you might be interested in and call them to learn how their job openings are announced. Listings might be posted in public libraries, colleges and universities, post offices, Job Service offices, and personnel offices of the various government units. Many of these positions are civil service positions and require applicants to take civil service tests or to follow complex application procedures which may prolong the hiring process-

Newspaper Articles

Read your newspaper to discover job opportunities. Watch for articles on business startups and expansions. This usually indicates that employers are either hiring now or will be hiring in the near future. Don't wait to see a help-wanted ad in the newspaper; follow up on these leads immediately.

Television/Radio

As a public service, some TV and radio stations will announce job openings that employers have available. Check with your local stations to see if they have this service available since this varies from area to area.

There are many ways of searching for a job. Do not rely on just one source. Using more than **one source will increase your chances of finding a job. Listed below are some suggested sources of job** leads:

People You Know

Many job seekers find employment by following leads from people they know. Following is a list of people that might provide job leads for you:

Friends	Insurance agents
Relatives	Doctors
Christmas card lists	Lawyers
Classmates	Bankers
Cashiers	Friends of friends
Politicians	Job placement personnel
Business associates	Suppliers
Previous employers	Vendors
Previous co-workers	Clubs
Dentists	Organizations
Accountants	Teachers
Social acquaintances	Neighbors
Ministers	Acquaintances of any of these

Make contact with people!

Direct Employer Contacts

While contacting employers directly may be time-consuming, it can be productive. Use the **Yellow** Pages, Classified Directory of Wisconsin Manufacturers, Wisconsin Services Directory, and newspaper articles to find the names and addresses of local employers- Contact them by phone, resume, **or** in person and follow their instructions for applying. if an employer is not hiring, ask if **you** can complete an application for future openings. If this is not possible, ask if they know of other places that might be interested in your skills.

Newspaper Want-Ads

Some employers prefer the convenience of want-ad recruiting, but it is a common misconception that employers list all their openings in the newspaper- Employers may use different job titles for work you're interested in, so read all ads carefully. Ads which give a description of the job are usually **worthy** of follow up. **"No** experience needed" ads, "blind" ads with no employer's name, and **"work** wanted" ads placed by applicants are usually not as helpful in finding work

Job Service

The Public Employment Service is a state and federally funded agency which assists people in looking for employment. There are thousands of local Job Service offices across the United States- Job Service matches applicants with job openings based on qualifications using a computerized matching system. Job Service has the largest source of job openings on a daily basis. In addition to providing job referrals to employers with job openings, Job Service may have counseling, testing, job search workshops and special group services available. **All** services are free of charge.

Entrepreneurship

If **you** are thinking about starting **your own** business, there may be affordable help available through your local Service Corps of Retired Executives (S.C.0-R.E.) chapter and the Small Business Association (S-B-A.)- Man colleges and universities have business outreach centers that may be able to help you. Your local library, Job Service, **or** Chamber of Commerce may be able to provide useful information also.

Other

Check bulletin boards at **grocery** stores, churches, schools. Etc. Follow upon "Help Wanted" signs.

Call or visit your local Chamber of Commerce. Watch for new construction.

Join a professional or trade association and network with members for information on opportunities.

Check with local non-profit, community-based organizations about employment services they might have available-

Register with your local union hiring hall-

Call telephone job information hot lines-

Getting a job is a job in itself and you should be prepared to really work at it. Developing and checking out as many job opportunities as possible can make your job search a productive experience!!

Success in your career depends on your drive, personality, ability to make contacts, motivation and experience (education)

"Don't let weed grow around your dreams, goals, desires and vision." Be open to new ideas, areas. Be guided in selecting a career.

List of Open Ended Questions and **Directives**

What skills do you bring to this job?

How would your last boss describe you?

Which of your jobs did you like most?

Why do you want to work here?

How would you handle ---- situation?

What is your favorite part of your last position?

Why did you leave your last employer?

Tell me about your experience with this type of work.

Share with us your strengths and weaknesses.

Describe what you would consider the perfect job.

Others:

DRIVE

Some people seem to be propelled by an internal

engine that never quits. Whatever they start,

they finish. And when they finish, they start

something else. That's drive. If you have it,

consider yourself fortunate: it's a gift that can

rocket you to the top. If you don't have it,

don't worry about it: just visualize what you

want, then go after it with all your heart.

A word of caution: know the difference between

having drive and being driven. Don't let life's

pressures steer you away from your values,

or you could be headed for a crash.

Always remember you're in the driver's seat!

Written by Rick Bayan

Other Sources: You May Find it Helpful To Dowse Through Some of these Reference Materials for More Ideas.

Allen, Jeffrey The Career Trap: Breaking Through the 10 year Barrier to get the Job you Really Want. New York: AMACOM, 1995.

Bly, Robert W. and Blake, Gary Dream Jobs: A guide to tomorrow's top careers. New York, J Wiley. 1985.

Bolles, Richard Nelson What Color is Your Parachute. Berkeley, CA: Ten Speed Press, 1999.

Camenson Blythe Careers For Health Nuts And Others Who Like To Stay Fit. Lincolnwood, Illinois, 1996.

Caple, John   Finding The Hat That Fits: How To Turn Your Heart's Desire Into Your Life's Work. New York: Lune, 1993.

Daloz, Laurent Common Fire: Lives of Commitment in a Complex World. Boston: Beacon Press, 1996.

Faux, Marian The Complete Resume Guide. MacMillan USA, 1995.

Hirsch, Arlene Love Your Work and Success Will Follow: A Practical Guide to Achieving Total Career Satisfaction. NY: John Wiley, 1996.

Jackson, Tom ˙Not just another job: how to invent a career that works for you - now and in the future . New York: Times Books, 1992.

Krannichi, Ronald, Krannichi, Caryl Rae Jobs for people who love travel. Manassas Park, VA: Impact Publications, 1995.

Lauber, Daniel Non-Profit's Job Finder. River Forest IL: Planing Communications, 1994.

McAdam, Terry Careers In The Non-Profit Sector: Doing Well By Doing Good. Washington DC: Taft Group ,1986.

Ferris, Donna The Practical Job Search Guide: Your action plan to finding the right job in Today's Market. Ten Speed Press: Berkeley CA, 1996.

Michelozzi,Betty Neville   Coming Alive From Nine to Five: A career Search Handbook. Mayfield Pub Co: Mountain View CA, 1992.

Rogers, Roxanne Get a Job You Love. Chgo:Dearborn Financial Pub Inc., 1996.

APPENDIX

Who Am I
The Path I Have Walked So Far

(Complete this form. If you have more to add, use an extra sheet of paper.)

1. Name:_____

2. Birthdate:_____

3. Telephone/FAX/email:_____

4. Address(es):_____

5. Place of Birth:_____

6. Culture/Race/Ethnicity:_____

7. Parents/Grandparents/Guardians_____

_____

8. Siblings_____

9. Marriage/Relationships/Divorce/Separation_____

_____

10. In-laws/significant Family Members/Blood/non-blood relations_____

_____

11. Children (natural born, adopted, step-, god-)_____

_____

12. Grandchildren:_____

_____

13. Death of Significant People:_____

14. Significant People Who Have Affected You (+/-)_____

_____

15. Religious/Spiritual Belief Systems _____

16. Health/Medical/Conditions _____

_____

17. Education (all) _____

18. Work Experience/Occupation/Career _____

_____

19. Financial Situation (savings, debts, real estate, insurance, etc.) _____

_____

20. Leisure/Hobby/Sports _____

_____

21. Places of importance/significance (-/+) _____

_____

22. Features of Society that Concern You _____

_____

23. Government/Political/Social Organizations _____

_____

24. Media/Public Relations _____

25. Violence/Crime/Abuse/Neglect _____

_____

26. Special Events/Holidays _____

_____

27. Animals/Plants/Mineral Kingdom _____

28. Past Lives - also Fears/Habits/ Patterns/Cycles/[Ego: alter, material, spiritual] _____

Issue Record Balance Sheet

Name _____   Birthdate _____   Address _____   Phone _____

Follow steps 1-9

Pages 13-14	Page 18	Page 19	Page 20	Page 20	Page 21	Page 21	Page 30	Page 31
1. Who Am I!? (pages 8&9) Habits Fears Patterns	2. Level of Consciousness	3. Manifestation	4. Who	5. Time	Emotional Gauge 6A. Negative Pages 22-25	for HHH Dowsing 6B. Positive Pages 26-28	7. Resolution	8. 100% Balance

Issue Record Balance Sheet

Name _____ Birthdate _____ Address _____ Phone _____

Follow steps 1-9

Pages 13-14	Page 18	Page 19	Page 20	Page 20	Page 21	Page 21	Page 30	Page 31
1. Who Am I? (pages 8&9) Habits Fears Patterns	2. Level of Consciousness	3. Manifestation	4. Who	5. Time	Emotional Gauge 6A. Negative Pages 22-25	for HHH Dowsing 6B. Positive Pages 26-28	7. Resolution	8. 100% Balance

LIFE'S PATH - SOUL MISSION

Write it out and record on RECORD SHEET II on page 44.

Dowse out if everything has been fulfilled in your life at this time. This gives you some clues where you are going.

1. **Physical** - food, clothing, health, home, automobile, furniture, travel, hobbies, leisure, sports, etc.

2. **Mental, emotional, intellect** - education (schooling) emotional, self worth, acceptance, etc.

3. **Spiritual** - tools, resources, religious, spiritual education, etc.

4. **Education** - schooling, certificates, medals. (Education, mental, physical, emotional, nutritional, religious, spiritual),etc.

5. **Family** - Grandparents, parents, siblings, marriage, in-laws, children, grandchildren, etc.
Spiritual, Children of the World

6. **Financial**, savings, real estate, business, investment, pension, etc.

7. **Relationships** - female/male, animals, public, friendships, etc.

8. **Sexual** - sacred, unity. etc.

9. **Social** - work, experience, occupation, career, self expression, organization, technology, culture, events, etc.

For info: Please check the book TO OUR HEALTH, Using the Inner Art of Dowsing in the Search for Health-Happiness-Harmony

LIFE'S PATH - SOUL MISSION
Write it out record on Page 44

1. Self Discovery - Who Am I?
Finding my place and function in my Life's Mission.

2. What are my Goals, Dreams, Desires, Emotions, Vision , My life's Path, Soul Mission?

3. What did I achieve so far in my Life?

4. What do I want to achieve in my Life? spiritual/material - both?

"I must know what I am capable of, before I know where I am going with my Life's Path Soul Mission, lest I go nowhere at all."

5. What are my abilities? -Natural or acquired? Things I already do? Knowledge of my aptitudes - where I excel is the most important factor in selecting my Path Mission. Learning styles? What is for my Highest Good? What is fulfilling and rewards me as I deserve?

6. Am I capable of delegating, managing, negotiating, organizing, persuading, selling, supervising?

7. Am I skilled in the Art of Reasoning, simplifying, involving problems, drawing solutions, conclusions, information?

8. Am I able to help others, solve personal problems. Can I motivate others, advise, guide or counsel them? Nurturing.

9. Am I capable of serving people on a spiritual level? Emotional and Physical level?

10. What are my strengths? How Can I use them?

11. Am I doing this for myself, God, World, others, parents, partner, children.

12. What factors play an important role in my life?
    Is it marriage, children, parents, family, neighbors, sexuality, circle of friends, money, status, work, superiors, colleagues, hobbies, journeys, youth work, social assistance, health field, spirituality, etc. Material success, survival talents.

13. What are my tools - wisdom, drive, focus, responsibilities, commitment, direction, planning, High self esteem, trustworthy uniqueness, unconditional love

14. Do you strive or just survive?

15. Is your Life Mission/Vision heart directed?

CH-CH-CH-Changes - Chances

Give yourself an extra month each year to reach your goals. Simply eliminate the false mindset of "not enough time". Get up an extra half-hour early or go to bed a half-hour later each night (When you exercise more, eat better, and have positive reinforcing thought you may find that you can do with a half hour less sleep.) Use that time to either work on your goals or on yourself. It may not be much time in and of itself, but it sure adds up. A half-hour extra, six days a week, is three hours a week. That's 166 extra hours or more than four forty-hour work weeks extra per year!

FINDING YOUR LIFE'S PATH, YOUR SOUL MISSION

AWAKENING THE ME WITHIN Desire Goals Dreams Vision Interest Freedom Travel Choices Right Place Financial Freedom	People you want to be with	How much resources (i.e., time, money) do you want to give it	For whom? Self, family friends, world	Qualifications What skills, loves? Do I have these skills/interests? : managing negotiating supervising selling persuading organizing delegating guiding counseling Advising guiding counseling motivating nurturing serving drawing solutions simplifying information learning logic	To go back to school/change jobs	What do I gain? Creative expression, recognition new experiences Self esteem more life	Responsibilities Commitment Focus Direction Self esteem trust worthy uniqueness unconditional love	Activities	6th Sense Intuition Dowsing Gut feeling God Feeling

LIFE'S PATH SOUL MISSION

Balance is the key to wholeness.
Often the difference between a dream and a desire is simply getting it on paper.
<u>Write down</u> all the things you like to do and consider doing in your life what suits your soul.

Places to go

_____

People you want to know.

_____

Ways to change myself & the world

_____

Adventures/Cultures

_____

Books to read/to learn

_____

Crafts/sports I want to learn

_____

Religions, philosophies I want to study

_____

What did you like to do at different ages in your life

     1-10 years_____

     11-20 years_____

     21-30 years_____

     31-40 years_____

     41-50 years_____

     51-60 years_____

     beyond 61 years_____

Who do you like to be with (people)?

_____

Do you like to be alone, in a group with people, animals?

_____

What are your hobbies?

_____

Do you like to work(be of service) during the day or at night?

_____

Are you willing to reorganize your time?

_____

What are you willing to give up (time, money, being away from your family, friends, home, surroundings, country)?

_____

What are you willing to invest (time, money, Gifts you have)?

_____

Are you willing to go back to school (formal, informal, skill training)?

_____

Are you willing to change your occupation, take a lower paying job for you happiness?

_____

Are you willing to move to a different place?_____

Are you willing to commit drive, focus, be optimistic, put action behind it, go the distance, and
      be responsible._____

What are your responsibilities/commitments in your life at this time? What are the limits?

_____
_____
_____
_____

Define what do you really desire, want and dream of in your life.
You then set it into your subconscious mind and out to the Universe to manifest.

_____
_____
_____
_____

WRITE IT OUT ON PAPER VERY IMPORTANT!!!!!

The Force (God) Spirit is within you.
That Force is there to find your desires, your growth (Development)

NOW PLAN

What do you want to be when you grow up? Making plans - go where you are called
A carpenter, a house engineer, a star, a beggar, a spiritual leader, etc. Desires - do the things you love Make a list of your desires, dreams, goals, vision Find your occupation, career, job, owning your own business.   Look in the back pages of this book and dowse what is for your/God's highest good and for the good of all

"Listen to your heart and know that the work of self change is progressing in your life."

Relax, remember this is something you are doing for your self (Soul, God)

Desire List

Short Term	1 month	1 year	5 years	10 years or more
Clean closet write to people read a book watch a movie make a phone call	Put $5.00 in your bank account Help others with food, etc.	Find a partner make a commitment buy a car travel have a family	buy a house retire early	Live in another country

You can create and have everything you choose, Work it and make it work for you.

Write down all the things you considered doing in you life. Which suits your nature. Is this a 10, 9, 8 for the next two years? Then dowse out what # it is. You want to shoot for a 10 or 9.
You Know #10 is for your Highest Good
#9 is Very Good
#8 is Good
#7 is OK - don't sell yourself short - Not enough energy here.

Things I'd Like to Do	Rating

What I am is God's Gift to me. What I make of myself is my Gift to God

Success from Dr. Robert Schuller

4 P's
1. **Purpose**
2. **Passion - Enthusiasm**
3. **Principles**
4. **Partnership (God/Truth)**

If you get to where you're going, where will it be?
What I be, is up to me

ACCEPTANCE CHART

Yet it is not the past that reveals your direction, but the purpose with which you move.
The Third Millennium.

NOTES

NOTES